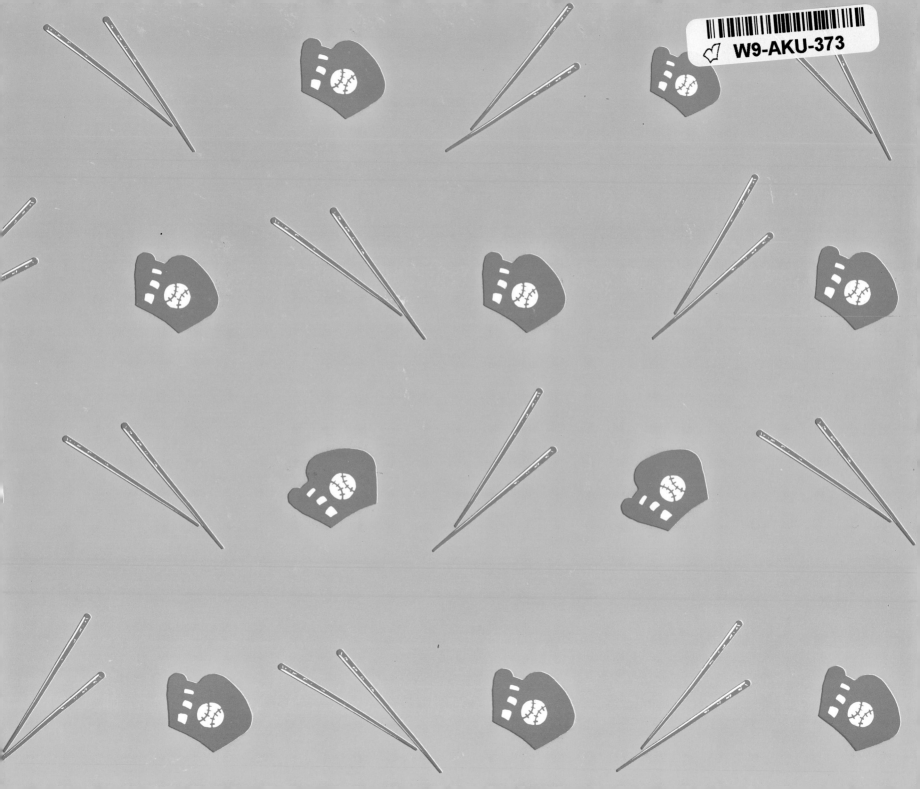

Katie-Bo

An Adoption Story

Library of Congress Cataloging-in-Publication Data
Fisher, Iris L.
   Katie-Bo : an adoption story.
   Summary: Relates the adoption of a Korean baby girl into an American family as seen through the eyes of her brother-to-be.
   [1. Adoption — Fiction. 2. Family life — Fiction]
I. Schaer, Miriam, ill. II. Title.
PZ7.F5327Kat   1987   [E]   87-19278
ISBN 0-915361-91-4

Typography by Quad Right
Photography by Aldo Mauro

Printed in Israel
Adama Books, 306 West 38 Street, New York, New York 10018

Katie-Bo

An Adoption Story

by Iris L. Fisher

Illustrated by Miriam Schaer

ADAMA BOOKS

New York

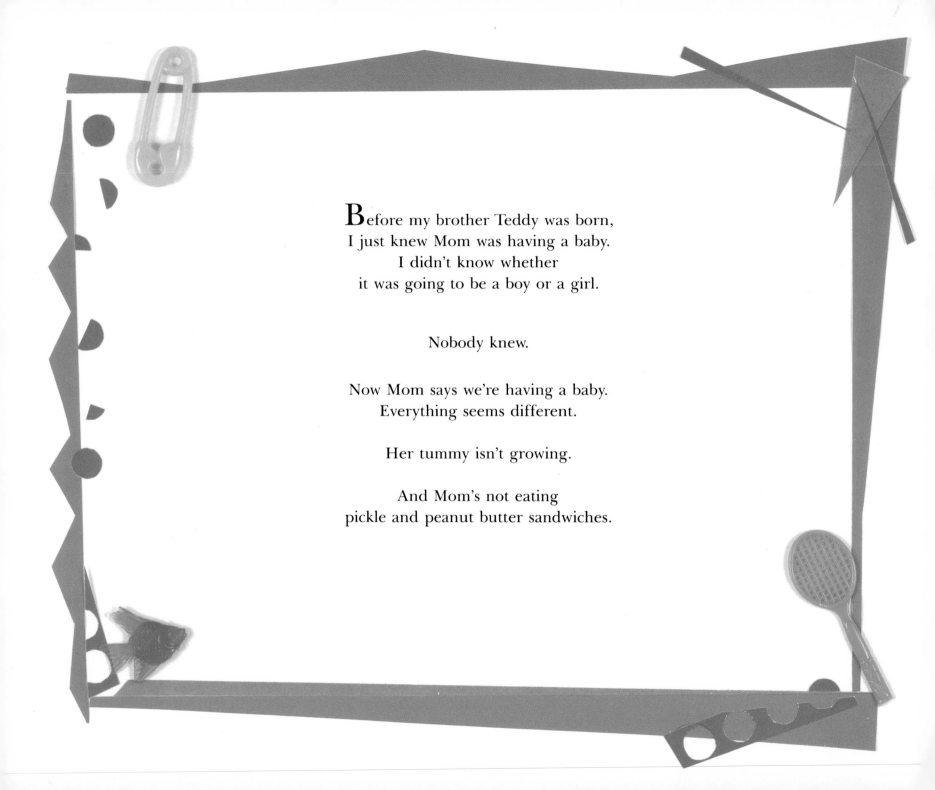

Before my brother Teddy was born,
I just knew Mom was having a baby.
I didn't know whether
it was going to be a boy or a girl.

Nobody knew.

Now Mom says we're having a baby.
Everything seems different.

Her tummy isn't growing.

And Mom's not eating
pickle and peanut butter sandwiches.

Mom says that we are adopting.

Daddy explains that adoption
is a very special way to have a baby.

Of course, our baby is growing in *a* mommy's tummy
but not *our* mommy's tummy.
Dad says that some women
who love their babies very much
can't always take care of them.

Our Mom says that it's because the lady
loves her baby so much that she
goes to an adoption agency.
That's a place where special people
called social workers look for a happy family like ours
to love and care for the baby forever.

We talk about adopting a baby sister.

We feel sad for the lady
whose baby we're going to adopt,
but happy for us.

Mommy and Daddy go to the Adoption Agency
to talk with Mrs. Blossom, our social worker.

They talk about what would be best
for our baby and what would
be best for all of us.

Soon after, Mrs. Blossom comes to our house.

She asks us how we feel about adopting a sister.

We tell her GREAT.

Dad and Mom tell us that our baby
may look a little different than Teddy and me.

We have fun drawing her picture.

Our baby is coming from Korea.
That's a far-away country.

We try to learn everything we can about Korea.

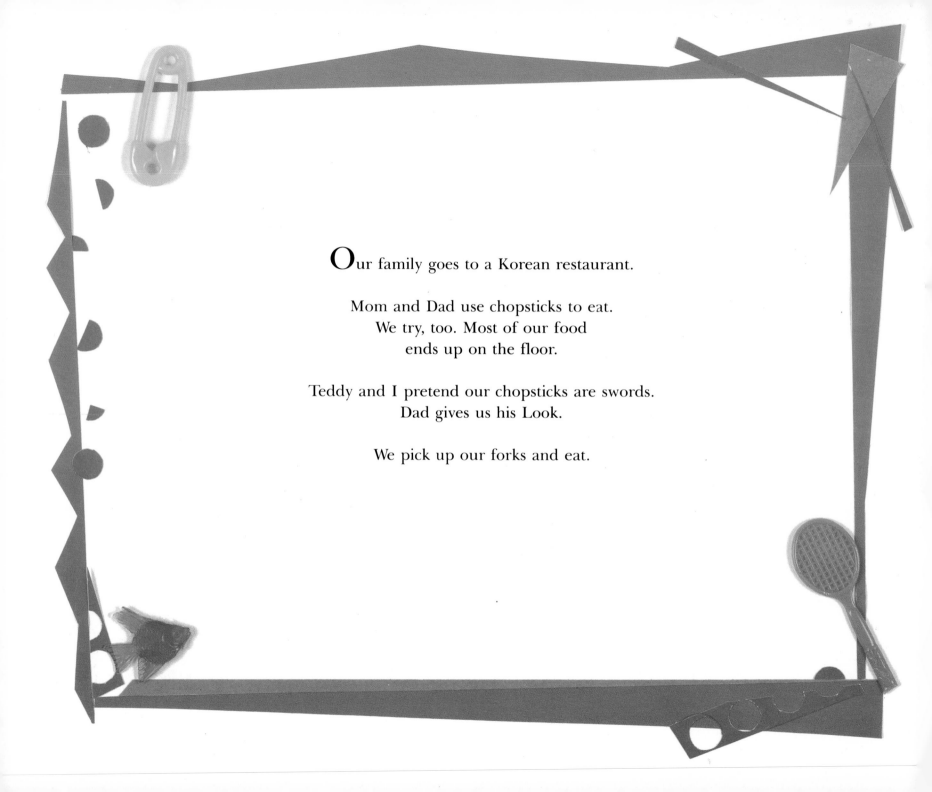

Our family goes to a Korean restaurant.

Mom and Dad use chopsticks to eat.
We try, too. Most of our food
ends up on the floor.

Teddy and I pretend our chopsticks are swords.
Dad gives us his Look.

We pick up our forks and eat.

Mrs. Blossom calls to tell us
that a picture of our baby has just arrived.

We get excited.

Tigger runs away.

Ted chases Daisy.

I chase Ted.

Everything shakes.

Dad and Mom go to see Mrs. Blossom.

They bring the baby's picture home.

She's two months old.

Our baby does look different.
She has brown hair and brown eyes.
And she's cute.

Our baby's Korean name is Bo Hee.
That means Treasure Delight.

My name is Jim.
Dad once said that means Wild One.

Mom and Dad fix up
the extra room with a crib and toys.

It sure looks different from my room.
There's no mess.

Teddy decides to draw
some cats and mice on the wallpaper.

Everyone says that Ted is a great artist.

Mom walks in. She sees the drawings.

She cries.

Dad yells.

Teddy screams.

Teddy says no one loves him.
Mom and Dad only love the baby.

Dad sends Ted to his room.

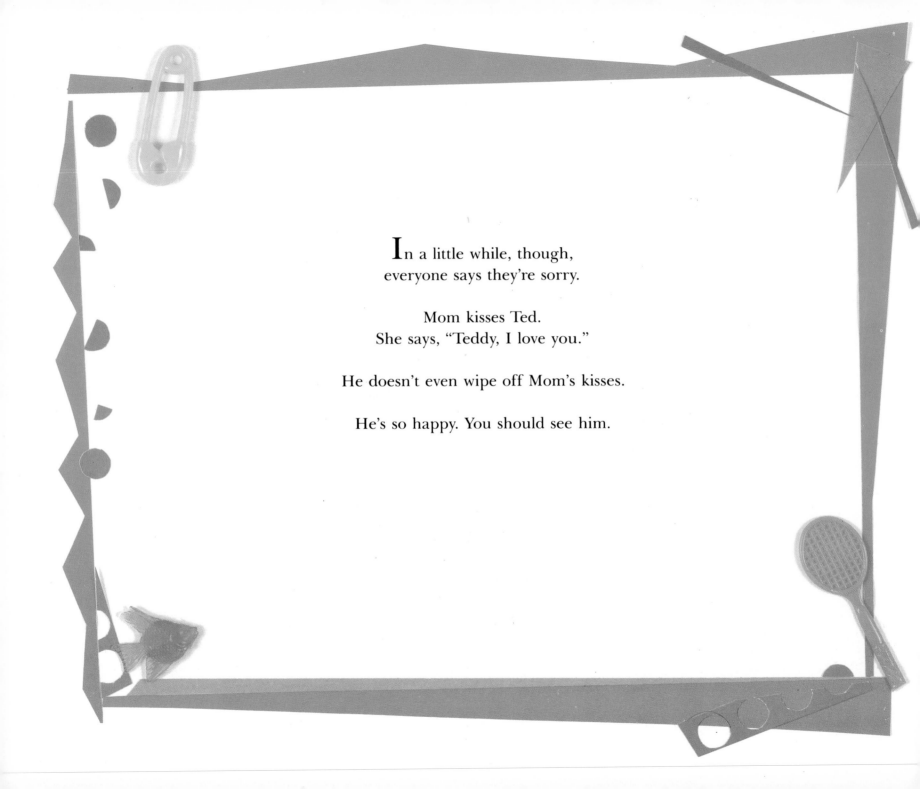

In a little while, though,
everyone says they're sorry.

Mom kisses Ted.
She says, "Teddy, I love you."

He doesn't even wipe off Mom's kisses.

He's so happy. You should see him.

We think our sister should have
an American name and a Korean name.

We look through lots of baby books
to find a name we all love.

We decide on Katie.

Our baby's name will be Katie-Bo.

They sound great together.

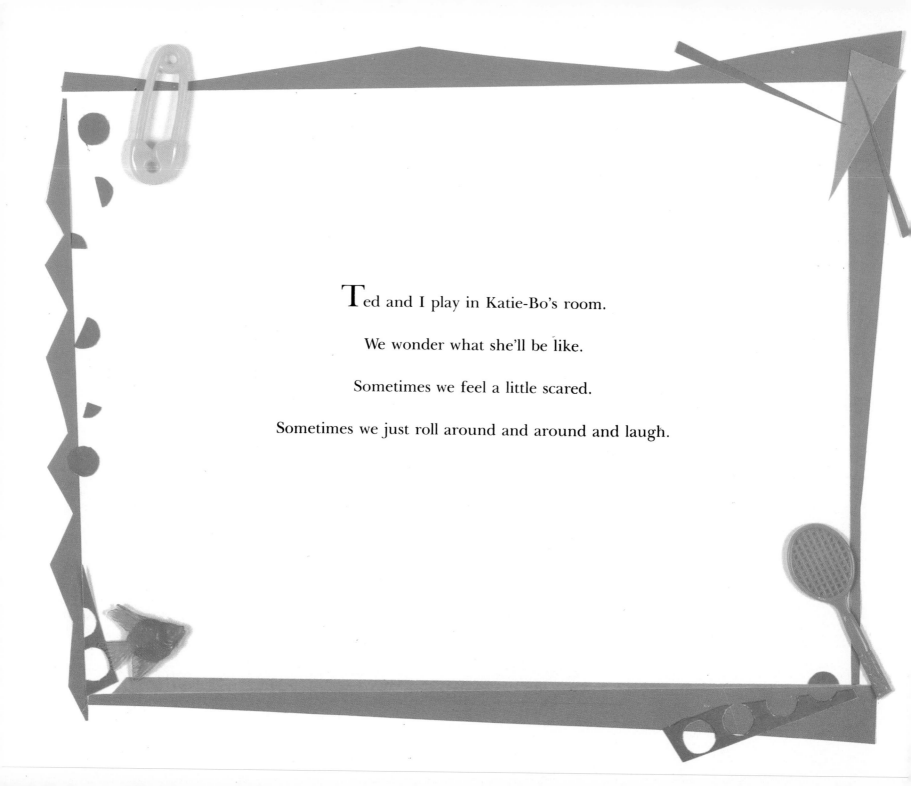

Ted and I play in Katie-Bo's room.

We wonder what she'll be like.

Sometimes we feel a little scared.

Sometimes we just roll around and around and laugh.

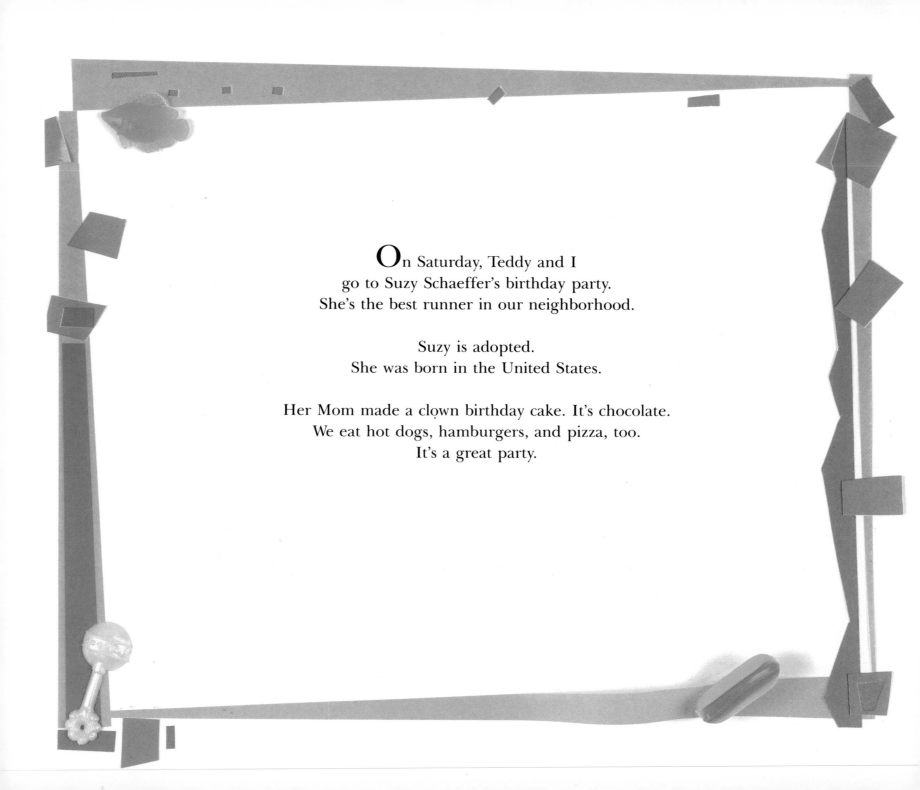

On Saturday, Teddy and I
go to Suzy Schaeffer's birthday party.
She's the best runner in our neighborhood.

Suzy is adopted.
She was born in the United States.

Her Mom made a clown birthday cake. It's chocolate.
We eat hot dogs, hamburgers, and pizza, too.
It's a great party.

At Katie-Bo's first birthday party,
Teddy says he wants mom
to make a spaceship cake.

Katie-Bo is coming.

She's coming on a big silver plane.

Our baby is four months old.

We're waiting at the airport
and we're feeling a little nervous.

There are four other families
waiting for their babies, too.
Everyone is showing pictures and telling stories.

When the man on the loudspeaker
says the plane from Korea is in,
everyone stops talking.

Mom and Dad put their arms around us.

My heart is bumping so much,
I'm sure all the people can hear it.

Teddy keeps squeezing my hand. Hard.

The babies are taken off the plane one at a time.

Mrs. Blossom brings out Katie-Bo.
We know our baby is special.

She has the biggest smile we've ever seen.

Mrs. Blossom gives Katie-Bo to us.

Mom starts to cry. Dad does, too.
Grown-ups sometimes cry when they're happy.

We take lots of pictures.

Teddy and I feel happy to have a little sister.

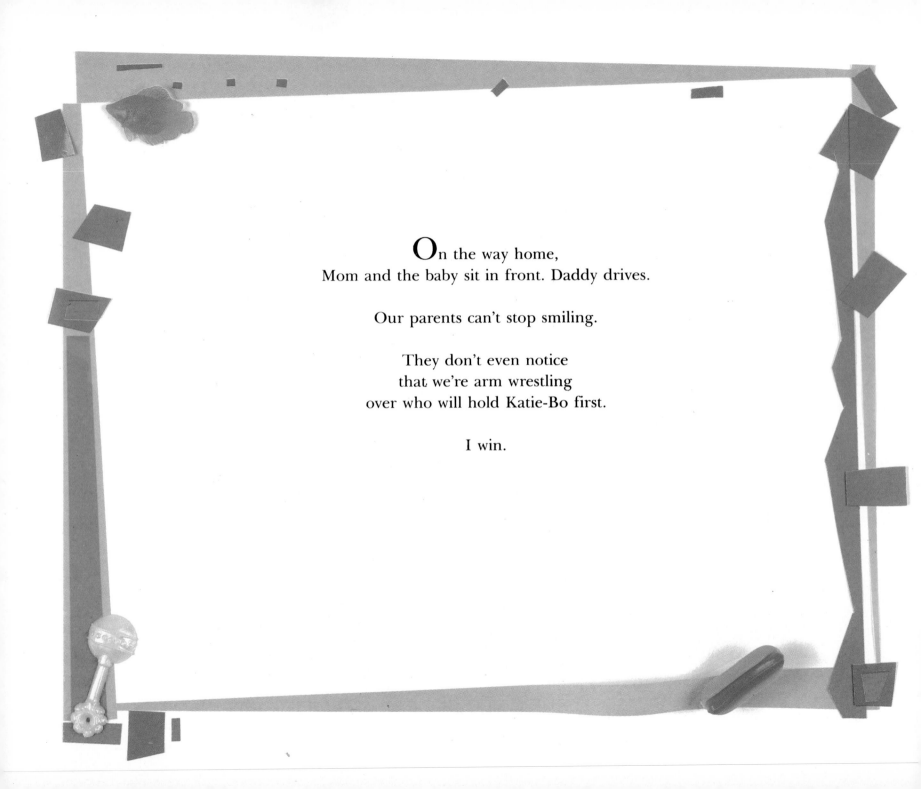

On the way home,
Mom and the baby sit in front. Daddy drives.

Our parents can't stop smiling.

They don't even notice
that we're arm wrestling
over who will hold Katie-Bo first.

I win.

We get to our house
and there are balloons all over the place.

On our front door there is a big sign.

Mom reads, "Welcome, Katie-Bo."
She and Dad start to laugh and cry.
Even Teddy and I are feeling a little strange.

Though Katie-Bo has been with us for eight months,
Mom and Dad still go to adoption meetings.

This time Mrs. Blossom came to our house
to see ALL of us.

She says we're a great family.

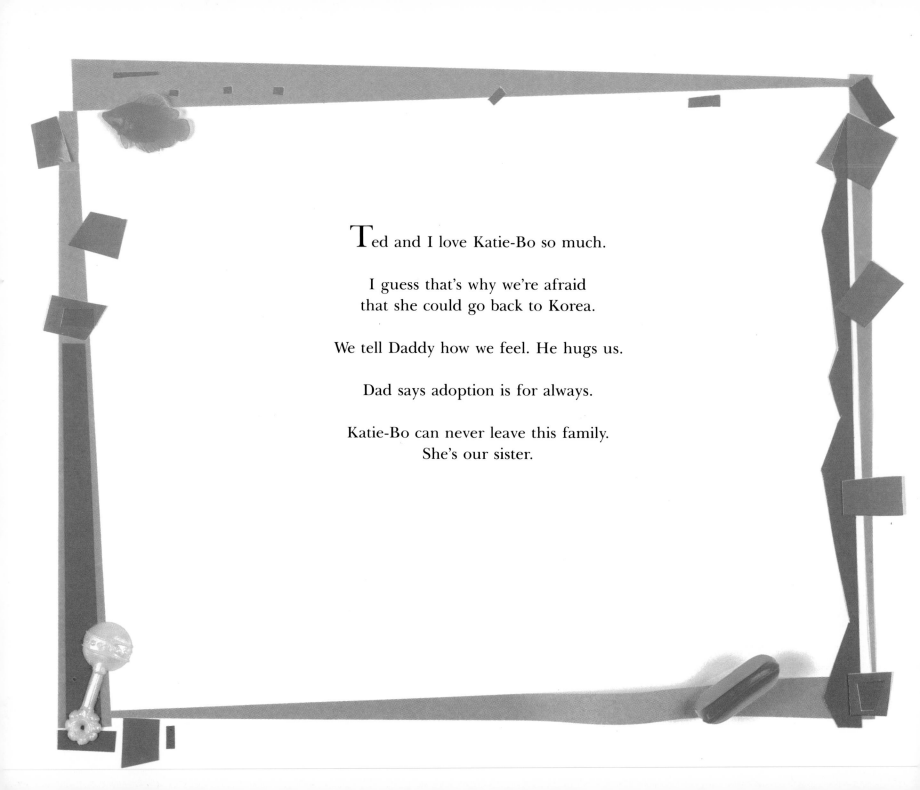

Ted and I love Katie-Bo so much.

I guess that's why we're afraid
that she could go back to Korea.

We tell Daddy how we feel. He hugs us.

Dad says adoption is for always.

Katie-Bo can never leave this family.
She's our sister.

We all go to visit Judge Delta.
He knows everything about adoption.

The judge holds Katie-Bo on his lap.
He says she's beautiful.

He isn't mad when she climbs on his desk
and throws his papers on the floor.
He says she's just a baby.

Judge Delta says Katie-Bo
is our sister forever.
Nothing can change that.

He signs special papers.
We all hug. Then we take pictures.

We have a big celebration.
Burgers, fries and milkshakes.

This is our best day ever.
We all agree – the whole family –
Mom, Dad, Ted, me,
and our forever sister, Katie-Bo.

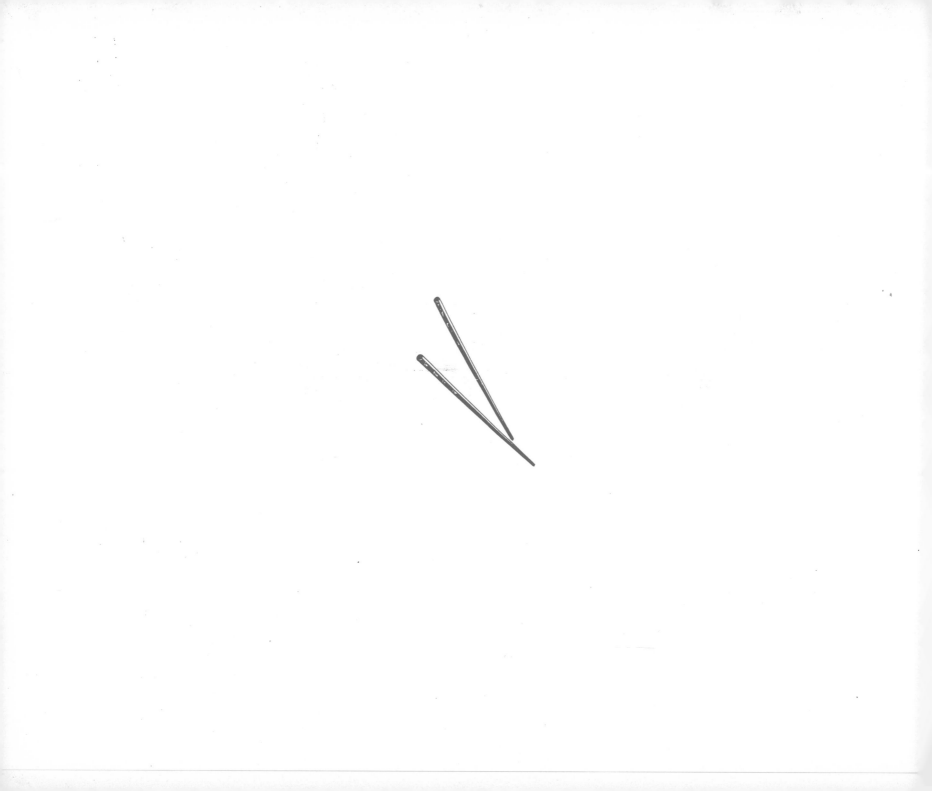

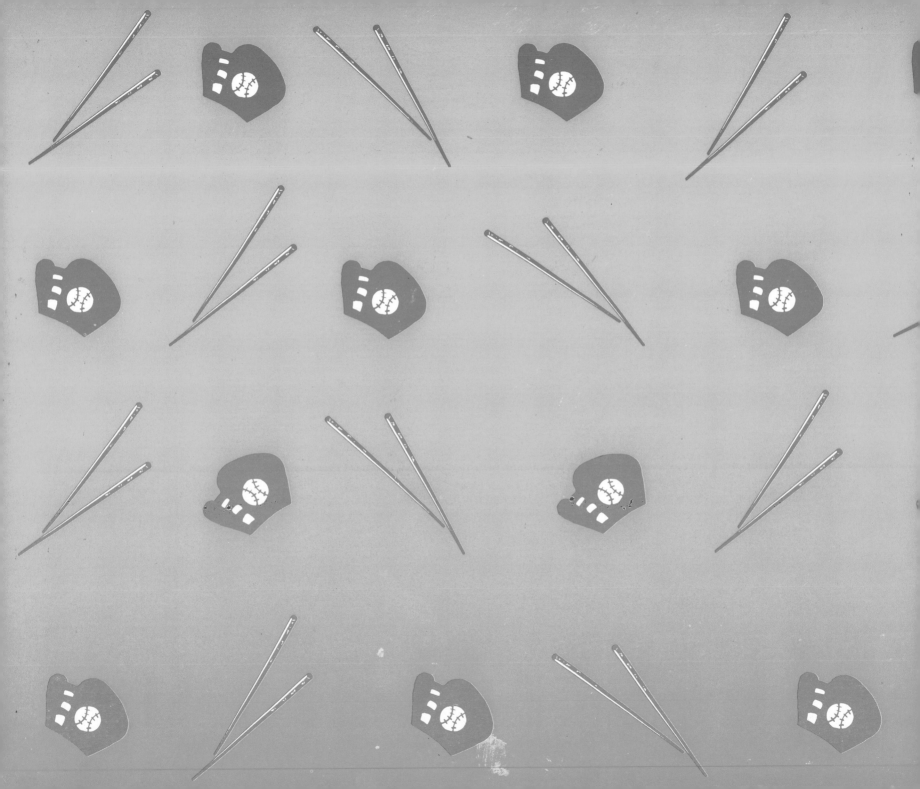